Fact Finders®

# →HOW LONG DOES IT TAKE TO MAKE A DIAMOND?

BY EMILY HUDD

**CONTENT CONSULTANT**

Dr. Uwe Richard Kackstaetter, Associate Professor,
Earth and Atmospheric Sciences, Metropolitan State
University of Denver

CAPSTONE PRESS
a capstone imprint

Fact Finders Books are published by Capstone Press,
1710 Roe Crest Drive, North Mankato, Minnesota 56003
www.mycapstone.com

**Library of Congress Cataloging-in-Publication Data**
Names: Hudd, Emily, author.
Title: How long does it take to make a diamond? / by Emily Hudd.
Description: North Mankato, Minnesota : Capstone Press, [2020] | Series: How
  long does it take? | Audience: Grades 4 to 6. | Includes bibliographical references and index.
Identifiers: LCCN 2018061086 (print) | LCCN 2019000908 (ebook) | ISBN
  9781543572995 (ebook) | ISBN 9781543572933 (hardcover) | ISBN
  9781543575385 (pbk.)
Subjects: LCSH: Diamonds--Juvenile literature. | Geophysics--Juvenile
  literature.
Classification: LCC QE393 (ebook) | LCC QE393 .H83 2020 (print) | DDC
  553.8/2--dc23
LC record available at https://lccn.loc.gov/2018061086

All internet sites appearing in back matter were available and accurate when this book was sent to press.

**Editorial Credits**
Editor: Marie Pearson
Designer and production specialist: Dan Peluso

**Photo Credits**
iStockphoto: joebelanger, cover (bottom), rgbdigital, cover (top); Newscom: Danita Delimont Photography, 5, James Borchuck, St Petersburg Times/ZumaPress, 26; Science Source: Andrew Lambert Photography, 11, Gary Hincks, 15, The Natural History Museum, London, 25, 28, Tom McHugh, 19; Shutterstock Images: Anneka, 17, Art of Life, 29, Bjoern Wylezich, 13, Imfoto, 20, Ralf Lehmann, 8, Siberian Art, 7, Tatiana Grozetskaya, 22

Design Elements: Red Line Editorial

# TABLE OF
# CONTENTS

Introduction
## The Hope Diamond. . . . . . . . . . . . . . . 4

Chapter One
## Deep in the Earth . . . . . . . . . . . . . . . . 6

Chapter Two
## How a Diamond Forms. . . . . . . . . . . 10

Chapter Three
## Coming to the Surface . . . . . . . . . . . 14

Chapter Four
## Discovery . . . . . . . . . . . . . . . . . . . . 18

Chapter Five
## Age and Shape . . . . . . . . . . . . . . . . 24


Glossary . . . . . . . . . . . . . . . . . . 30
Further Reading . . . . . . . . . . . . . . 31
Critical Thinking Questions . . . . . . . . 31
Internet Sites . . . . . . . . . . . . . . . . 31
Index. . . . . . . . . . . . . . . . . . . 32

# THE HOPE
# DIAMOND

A boy visits the National Museum of Natural History in Washington, D.C. He sees people crowded around something. A blue diamond shines underneath a light. It is the famous Hope diamond. It is bigger than any diamond he's seen. It is just under 1 inch (2.5 centimeters) long. It is about the size of a grape and weighs 45.52 **carats**. The diamond is on a necklace. Sixteen white diamonds form a circle around it.

Diamonds are precious **gems**.

**FACT**

Gems are weighed in carats just like people are weighed in pounds or kilograms. Five carats is equal to 0.04 ounces (1 gram).

carat—a unit to measure the weight of diamonds and gems

gem—a precious stone made from crystals

They are rare. This makes them hard to study. Diamonds grow very deep underground. Part of how they form is a mystery. Many diamonds found today are more than 1 billion years old, much older than the dinosaurs!

The Hope diamond is one of the most famous diamonds.

# CHAPTER ONE

# DEEP IN THE EARTH

Earth has three main layers. They include the crust, the mantle, and the core. The crust is a thin layer. It is only 25 miles (40 kilometers) thick. Humans live on the crust. It includes mountains and oceans. The core is the center of Earth. It is 4,330 miles (6,970 km) wide and extremely hot. The weight of all the rocks above squeezes it tightly from all sides.

The mantle is the layer between the crust and the core. It is about 1,800 miles (2,900 km) thick.

**FACT**
Scientists estimate that Earth's core is 10,800 degrees Fahrenheit (6,000°C). That is as hot as the surface of the sun.

The mantle is solid, but it can squish and move like modeling clay. In some places the rocks melt. This melted rock is called **magma**. Most diamonds form in the upper part of the mantle.

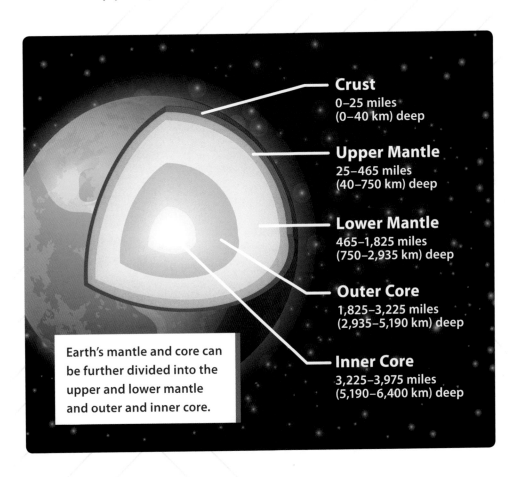

**Crust**
0–25 miles
(0–40 km) deep

**Upper Mantle**
25–465 miles
(40–750 km) deep

**Lower Mantle**
465–1,825 miles
(750–2,935 km) deep

**Outer Core**
1,825–3,225 miles
(2,935–5,190 km) deep

**Inner Core**
3,225–3,975 miles
(5,190–6,400 km) deep

Earth's mantle and core can be further divided into the upper and lower mantle and outer and inner core.

magma—a hot liquid that cools to lava and then to rock

Lava mainly comes from Earth's crust. Diamonds are formed deeper in Earth's mantle. Scientists cannot study the natural growing conditions there.

Diamonds need high pressure and high temperatures to form. Diamonds form more than 90 miles (145 km) below Earth's surface. At this depth the temperature is at least 2,000 degrees Fahrenheit (1,000 degrees Celsius). The weight of the outer layers of Earth create pressure in the mantle. The pressure is about 650,000 to 940,000 pounds (290,000–430,000 kilograms) per square inch (6.5 square centimeters). This is similar to the weight of 80 elephants standing on your toe! These **conditions** make the mantle the best place for diamonds to form.

**FACT**

Blue diamonds like the Hope form as deep as 410 miles (660 km) below Earth's surface. That is four times deeper than most other kinds of diamonds. Blue diamonds are extremely rare.

condition—the situation in which something is happening

# CHAPTER TWO

# HOW A DIAMOND FORMS

Diamonds are made of carbon **atoms**. Carbon is an element. It is found naturally in the ground. Carbon atoms bond together under high pressure and high temperatures. They also form other **minerals** like graphite. Graphite is used in pencil lead.

> **FACT**
> Diamonds are among the hardest minerals. Few other minerals can scratch them.

When forming a diamond, each carbon atom bonds to four other carbon atoms. The bonds make a pattern. The pattern is evenly spaced.

atom—the smallest unit of an individual element and the building block for all things on Earth

mineral—a material found in nature that is not an animal or plant

It is this special arrangement of atoms that makes it a diamond rather than just a lump of carbon. Diamonds are one of the hardest natural minerals in the world.

3-D models can show how carbon atoms (black circles) are arranged when making a diamond.

Diamonds grow as many carbon atoms join together. This group of atoms is called a crystal. Over time new carbon atoms can bond to the crystal to form new layers of diamond. The diamond continues to grow. One carat of diamond is billions of carbon atoms bonded together.

Diamonds are made deep in the earth. This makes them difficult to study. Scientists do not know how long it takes diamonds to grow naturally. It could be a few weeks or millions of years.

Scientists have studied diamonds to learn about them. They noticed diamonds can stop growing for a while and then start growing again.

Sometimes the temperature changes. Or there is no carbon to add. This stops the diamond crystal from growing. The process can pause for hundreds of years. However, the crystals continue growing when the conditions are right again.

Scientists don't know exactly how long it takes for a diamond to grow.

# CHAPTER THREE

# COMING TO THE SURFACE

Diamonds cannot travel from the mantle to the crust on their own. Most diamonds will spend their entire existence stuck deep in the mantle. The few diamonds people have seen have been caught up in volcanic **eruptions**. But these are not ordinary volcanic eruptions. They are special kinds of eruptions called kimberlites.

**FACT** Most diamonds scientists know of traveled to the surface within the last 500 million years.

Kimberlite is a type of rock deep in the mantle. There, kimberlite is magma.

eruption—a forceful, often violent, explosion that pushes lava, steam, or other matter onto Earth's surface

No one has seen a kimberlite erupt. But scientists have an idea of how these eruptions might work. Kimberlites erupt because of high pressure. The pressure causes layers above to crack. The cracks form **vertical** pipes. The kimberlite magma moves upward through the pipes. It picks up diamonds from the mantle. It carries the diamonds up to the surface along with other broken pieces of rocks.

A kimberlite pipe is shaped like a giant carrot. It goes deep through the crust and into the mantle.

vertical—angled up and down

Diamonds from kimberlite eruptions can travel 20 to 30 miles (30 to 50 km) per hour. That means they can get to the surface in a few hours. That speed is important. When diamonds are carried to the surface, they no longer have extreme pressure squeezing them. If a diamond were brought up more slowly, it might change from diamond to graphite. Graphite is another form of carbon that is more stable at Earth's surface.

## CHANGING TO GRAPHITE

Carbon atoms don't just make diamonds. They also make graphite. This soft black mineral is used in pencils. Carbon atoms in graphite form flat layers that are only weakly bonded together. The layers break apart easily. They leave a mark when rubbed on paper.

Graphite is a useful material for writing.

In a kimberlite eruption, Earth's temperatures are cooler closer to the surface. The kimberlite cools and hardens into solid rock. The last kimberlite eruption happened as recently as 11,000 years ago. But many happened millions of years ago. Most kimberlites are found in areas with the oldest rock on Earth. This includes Brazil, South Africa, and Australia. Earth's crust is very old in those locations.

# CHAPTER FOUR

# DISCOVERY

Finding diamonds is difficult. They are hidden beneath Earth's surface. But scientists have figured out ways to increase people's chances of finding diamonds. **Geologists** look for kimberlite rocks. They know diamonds might have been carried to the surface in these kinds of volcanic rocks. So far they have only found 6,400 kimberlites on Earth. Not all kimberlites contain diamonds. Fewer than 1 in 100 kimberlites have a diamond deposit in them. And kimberlite rocks are hard to find. So there are likely many more undiscovered diamond deposits.

Not all kimberlites have diamonds in them, but natural diamonds are always found in kimberlites.

Red garnets are indicator minerals, but they are also valuable gems.

One way to look for kimberlites that contain diamonds is to look for indicator minerals. These are clues that diamonds might be nearby.

Deep red garnets are an example of an indicator mineral. Indicator minerals are more common than diamonds, so they are easier to find. Red garnets and other indicator minerals can form next to diamonds in the mantle. They can also travel to the surface in kimberlites along with diamonds. If scientists find indicator minerals, they are on the right track to finding diamonds nearby.

Once scientists have found a spot with enough diamonds to make a profit, people can mine for them. Mining for diamonds is expensive and takes time. Diamond mining companies have different ways of mining depending on the location.

Kimberlite mines look like massive funnels. They can damage natural habitats.

To mine kimberlite pipes, companies dig deep holes in the pipes. They collect loads of rock and dirt. The collection is taken to a special building. Machines break the rock into small pieces. Machines **sift** through the rock and dirt.

sift—to look through and separate big pieces from small ones

Diamonds repel water. But they attract grease. The rock mixture is shaken on a table coated in grease. The diamonds stick to the grease. Rock and soil do not.

Some companies mine riverbanks. Diamonds can travel in water and rivers to new locations. Mining in water is complicated. Companies build walls that change the flow of the water. The area is cleared of water. Then machines dig into the riverbank. Soil and rock are collected. They are taken to a special building and checked for diamonds.

**FACT**

The public can dig for diamonds in Crater of Diamonds State Park. The park is in Murfreesboro, Arkansas. The most valuable diamond ever found in the United States, the Esperanza, was found there in 2015. It is worth $1 million.

# AGE AND SHAPE

As a diamond grows and gets larger, it can sometimes grow around another mineral grain. The mineral gets trapped inside the diamond. It is called an **inclusion**. Some minerals contain elements that **decay** slowly over time. They change from one material to another. They change at a steady rate. Scientists can use these elements to find out how old the minerals are. This gives scientists an idea of when the inclusion became trapped in the diamond. That date gives them a clue to the diamond's age.

## DATING THE HOPE DIAMOND

The Hope diamond was found in India. Scientists studied the kimberlite rocks around it to estimate its age. The rocks were 1.2 billion years old. That means the Hope diamond is at least 1.2 billion years old.

Scientists can also study the rocks found near a diamond to figure out its age. Diamonds are very old. They range in age. The oldest diamonds are 3.5 billion years old. The youngest are less than 100 million years old.

Diamonds can have garnet inclusions.

Not all diamonds formed millions or billions of years ago. Scientists can grow some quickly in labs. In the 1950s, scientists learned how to make diamonds in labs. They made large machines that provided the right temperature and pressure for diamonds to grow.

Powerful machines can mimic the conditions a diamond would need to grow in Earth's mantle.

22

Modern machines are smaller. They are about the size of a

microwave. First, a small bit of diamond crystal is put inside. Second, carbon gas is added. Third, the machine heats up. The hot temperature causes the carbon atoms to bond to the diamond. The small diamond crystals grow. The machine cools quickly. The atoms keep their shape. A diamond has grown. The whole process can take up to 10 weeks.

Lab diamonds are often very small. Conditions are controlled, so they are purer than natural diamonds. They are useful for tools and devices that need to be very strong and accurate, such as machines that cut and drill strong materials.

Diamonds naturally grow in a basic diamond shape. But people shape the many flat surfaces seen in jewelry.

Natural diamonds are popular for use in jewelry. But diamonds don't naturally form into perfect, sparkling shapes. They begin as somewhat bumpy crystals.

Diamond cutters decide what shape to cut a diamond into. The flat, polished sides of the diamond are called facets. Diamond cutters rub a diamond with diamond powder, which acts like sandpaper, to make the facets. Magnifying glasses help them see small details. After the diamond is cut, they polish it. A spinning wheel polishes the facets. The diamond sparkles after it is polished.

Many people enjoy having diamond jewelry. It can be millions or billions of years old. Some people are willing to pay a lot for diamonds because of the gem's history and beauty.

Diamonds make beautiful pieces of jewelry.

# GLOSSARY

**atom** (AH-tum)—the smallest unit of an individual element and the building block for all things on Earth

**carat** (KAR-uht)—a unit to measure the weight of diamonds and gems

**condition** (kon-DIH-shun)—the situation in which something is happening

**decay** (di-KAY)—to break down over a certain time

**eruption** (i-RUHP-shun)—a forceful, often violent, explosion that pushes lava, steam, or other matter onto Earth's surface

**gem** (JEM)—a precious stone made from crystals

**geologist** (jee-AH-luh-jist)—a person who studies rocks and is an expert on them

**inclusion** (in-KLOO-shun)—a mineral trapped inside a diamond

**magma** (MAG-ma)—a hot liquid that cools to lava and then to rock

**mineral** (MIN-ur-uhl)—a material found in nature that is not an animal or plant

**sift** (SIFT)—to look through and separate big pieces from small ones

**vertical** (VER-ti-kuhl)—angled up and down

# ADDITIONAL RESOURCES

## FURTHER READING

**Callery, Sean, and Miranda Smith**. *Rocks, Minerals & Gems*. New York: Scholastic, 2016.

**Machajewski, Sarah**. *Digging for Diamonds*. Gemstones of the World. New York: PowerKids Press, 2018.

**Oxlade, Chris**. *Minerals*. Rock On! Chicago: Heinemann Raintree, 2016.

## CRITICAL THINKING QUESTIONS

1. Some diamonds are grown in labs. Others formed millions or billions of years ago in Earth's mantle. Which sort of diamond do you prefer? Why? Why do you think other people might prefer the other type of diamond?

2. Diamonds are made deep in the earth. In your own words, describe how they form and travel to the surface. Use evidence from the text to support your answer.

3. Diamonds found today are as old as 1 to 3 billion years. What is one way scientists can learn about the age of a diamond?

## INTERNET SITES

**DK Find Out! Diamond**
https://www.dkfindout.com/us/earth/crystals-and-gems/diamond/

**National Geographic Kids: Diamond**
https://kids.nationalgeographic.com/explore/science/diamond/#diamonds-raw.jpg

**Smithsonian: The Hope Diamond**
https://www.si.edu/spotlight/hope-diamond

# INDEX

age, 5, 24–25, 27, 29
Australia, 17

blue diamonds, 4, 9
Brazil, 17

carats, 4, 12, 27
carbon, 10–13, 16, 27
core, 6, 7
Crater of Diamonds
    State Park, 23
crust, 6, 7, 14, 17
crystals, 12–13, 27, 28

diamond cutters, 29
dinosaurs, 5

Esperanza diamond, 23

garnets, 21
geologists, 18
graphite, 10, 16

Hope diamond, 4, 9, 25

inclusions, 24
indicator minerals,
    20–21

kimberlites, 14–17,
    18–22, 25

lab diamonds, 26–27

magma, 7, 14–15
mantle, 6–9, 14–15, 21
minerals, 10–11, 16,
    20–21, 24
mining, 21–23

National Museum of
    Natural History, 4

pressure, 9, 10, 15, 16, 26

South Africa, 17

temperature, 9, 10, 13,
    17, 26–27

## ABOUT THE AUTHOR

Emily Hudd is a full-time children's author who loves writing nonfiction on a variety of topics. She lives in Minnesota with her husband.